INTRODUCTION TO AFFILIATE MARKETING FOR BEGINNERS:

The Ultimate Guide to Starting Your Affiliate Marketing Journey and Earning Passive Income.

Thomas S. Birch

Table of Contents:

INTRODUCTION TO AFFILIATE MARKETING FOR BEGINNERS

A powerful sales staff is one of the ways that a company may expand its operations. Creating your own sales force used to be a highly costly endeavour, and as a result, it established a significant barrier to entry for those who were in the business of creating products. You are able to not only become a salesman yourself for a wide variety of goods and creators, but you are also able to build your own things to sell yourself, which is a wonderful development that has been made possible by the development of remarkable internet monitoring technology.

Building a sales force that can bring in multiple six figures and even millions of dollars can also be accomplished via the use of affiliate technology. This can be accomplished without the need to hire staff. It is only when they make a sale that you pay your sales force, often known as your affiliates. The only way for you to gain money as an affiliate (salesperson) is if you really make a sale.

It is, in fact, as easy as it possibly can be. However, before you go headfirst into affiliate marketing, it is a smart idea to educate yourself as much as possible on the subject. You will be able to take your company to the next level and get closer to being the genuine CEO of your company if you educate yourself on affiliate marketing and the different methods in which you can maximise your revenue.

In order to be successful in earning money via affiliate marketing, you will need to identify your niche, find the appropriate items to promote, develop your own products, locate the appropriate affiliates to sell those products, and maintain the motivation of your affiliates. It all begins with finding and understanding your specialty.

Chapter 1

DISCOVERING YOUR NICHE

The very first thing you need to do if you want to earn money as an affiliate marketer - whether you're going to make money selling other people's goods or your own (best to do both) - is that you need to figure out who you want to work with and what niche you want to be part of.

• Who Do You Want to Work With?
One method to figure out the sort of individuals you'd want to work with or serve is to search inside yourself to identify your hobbies and passions. If you truly love being with certain individuals and you know about their aspirations, wants, and requirements due to being part of that audience yourself, that's one method to achieve it since you will already have insight.

However, don't allow this offer you an excuse not to complete your study. Your experiences, even as part of your specialized audience, are subjective and true outcomes may be substantially different than you expect. Try expressing your ideal consumer in one or two phrases to assist you go ahead.

• Who Is Now Serving That Audience?
Once you have discovered a prospective niche audience, it usually helps to look at the competition. After all, if this niche has no competitors, is it truly a viable niche?
Some people would advise that you should go for the low competition niches, but it's better to go for the niche that gives enough prospective clients for you to meet your revenue objectives if your conversion rate reaches industry norms.
For example, if there are 1000 prospective consumers, and according to your study there is a 4 to 7 percent conversion rate, and you know that you can get your materials and information in front of those 1000 clients, you may obtain at most 70 customers from a campaign. Is your pricing point high enough for those 70 customers to make you profitable?

• What Skills and Solutions Can You Provide To This Market?

Do you have specific education, experience, or information that makes you particularly fit for this niche? You don't have to be part of the audience to perform well in a niche.

For example, if you have found a niche that requires someone to advise them on products to utilize for their love of camping which are distinct from what's out there, you can still learn about it and assist the audience even if you have no camping experience or enjoyment of camping. Maybe instead of firsthand experience, you have resources that allow you to hire experts with subject matter knowledge to create your firm.

• What Distinguishes You?

Always look at yourself too. What makes you distinct from your competition?

What talents can you provide to this niche that others can't? How can you stand out from the crowd? Are you going to tackle the niche in a different manner than the others? For example, if you're a business coach, are you buttoned up or a free spirit? Whatever you are, you're going to draw a completely different section of your audience base than someone who is different from you.

• Look Via An Affiliate Network For Products That Cater To That Audience
The second thing you want to do is ensuring that whatever topic you select is lucrative.

Asking yourself whether it's lucrative is a crucial question. Just because you have internet and desire doesn't make it a viable niche. What makes it lucrative is that the target audience exists in adequate number and has enough money to acquire the solutions you build and supply.

Once you limit down some alternatives, the major factors are whether your niche concept is lucrative or not, and whether you have the abilities to continue or not - either skills you gain or talents you buy from others. Choose a niche that you enjoy that can give adequate profit and that you know how to service.

Chapter 2

FINDING THE RIGHT PRODUCT OR SERVICE TO PROMOTE

Now that you know who your audience is and the category you want to be part of, it's time to discover the suitable items and/or services to market to them. There are numerous methods of locating the items or services to market to your audience.

• Issues and Solutions

Once you have a sense of who your audience is, you can concentrate on finding out their problems and then seeking ways to address them. Make a list of at least three problems that you wish to address for the audience, depending on the niche you've chosen.

Here is an example:

1. Audience: Married working parents with school-aged children who thrive on order

2. Problems: Keeping a family schedule, food planning, arranging

3. Potential Solutions: Digital calendars, DFY meal planning and shopping lists, organization suggestions and organization items

Once you have a list of challenges and answers, go to several renowned affiliate networks to search for the items you have identified as a suitable match.

A short search on ClickBank.com - a renowned affiliate network where you can locate items in any sector to sell as well as utilize to promote your own products - reveals various products that you may wish to promote, such as Get Organized

Now

Don't simply start pushing it now, however. Make a list of various goods. Then, do some research on each product. Find information about the creator, look at the conversion rate for the product, and consider about how the creator's beliefs and style fit well with the brand language you want to express.

If you don't know someone who knows them to testify for their professionalism, test them out by purchasing the goods yourself so that you can assess the quality of the product and the business for their customer service. After all, as an affiliate marketer, you are passing your consumers over to someone else to service. You need to make sure they will take excellent care of your consumers so that your audience continues to appreciate your suggestions.

• Various Programmes

There are various affiliate networks that feature chances for you to market to your audience. Each has its own idiosyncrasies and concerns that you'll have to learn about when you join a network. You may also discover affiliate items via direct programs which are not included in affiliate networks.

For example, many independent publishers appreciate employing technologies like aMember.com to build up their program, in which case they won't be included on the affiliate platforms.

To discover such items, just hunt for solutions using terms that you believe will find them.

For example, in the example above, we searched for Household Organization on ClickBank. Search for Household Organization on Google to find out what it displays.

The first result in our situation is a website named Getorganizedgal.com which provides solutions that the audience would need and desire.

However, you cannot notice an affiliate program, but after additional inquiry she utilizes Teachable to provide her courses. Teachable features an incorporated affiliate module. You could write her an email expressing how you enjoy her goods (after you purchase some) and that your audience will too if they create an affiliate program for you.

Another that pops up is Cozi.com, which is a family organizer. It features a calendar, grocery lists, to-do lists, recipes, and meal planner and even a family journal. You may promote Cozi and earn money via their affiliate program if you match the conditions.

A few programs to check out are:

4. JVZoo.com

5. Affilorama.com

6. ClickBank.com

7. ShareASale.com

8. Amazon Associates

9. eBay Partner Network

10.CJ Affiliate

11.Thrive Market

12.Udemy.com

13.Skillshare.com

Each network has its benefits and downsides, and there are many more than these. You may get vast listings of affiliate networks by searching Google for "affiliate networks," and you can also locate specialized networks. For example, if you wish to offer organic goods alone, you'll discover various possibilities.

You may also seek for particular items you'd want to promote, discover a link to their affiliate network, or contact them for information about it. Some company owners don't utilize affiliate networks, but so many do that you're guaranteed to discover numerous profitable goods that you can market. Even if you don't see one, you can still email the designer to offer your services by providing them your social proof.

• Establishing Profitability

Before you pick a product to market, it's vital that you check out whether the product is lucrative or not. If it's featured on an affiliate network, you can examine the stats mentioned to assist you assess how lucrative the product is. If you are working directly with a product creator, you may need to test your assumptions after checking out the product yourself.

Here are some things to think about.

14.High Commissions - When it comes to digital items, less than 50 percent commission is definitely a waste of time.

15.High Sales Price – If it's a commission lower than 50 percent, is the selling price high enough that you'd earn a per-sale price that makes it worth your time?

16. Conversion Rate – Most affiliate programs will have something to do with the conversion rate, how many sales have been made, or other statistics to help you assess whether this is a good decision or not.

17.Sales Page - What does the sales page look like? While it may not pleasure you to discover, the lengthier sales pages sell better than shorter ones for many audiences. Is the sales page planned out? Does it convert?

18.purchase It - When you locate a product that you believe you want to market to your audience, purchase the product. If you have enough influence, you may be able to get it free or a trial copy of some type for you to examine. However, buying it as a consumer is the greatest way to discover how they conduct business and whether the product is fit for your audience.

19.Is There Competition? – If you perform a search and discover other items like this one that you wish to market, that's a positive thing. You won't have to educate your market as much if it's already something they desire and are seeking for.

20.Can You Come Up with More Search Terms? - Once you have concluded that a product is something you want to promote, can you come up with more search phrases for it so that you can start generating content for marketing?

21.How Will You market This Product? – The second issue you want to ask yourself is how you'll market the product. Will you run an all-out campaign or are you going to slide it in as an in-content link on your blog? Will you promote it to folks already on your list? Which segment? The more you can plan out precisely how, when and where you're going to market the product, the more likely it is to be lucrative.

Finding a successful product isn't actually that hard if you've selected a suitable niche that has a healthy audience screaming for the answers they need to make their life better. It's your duty to find out what your niche is, the items your audience needs, and how you will deliver them to that audience.

You may also build your own items for the niche. Let's look at it next.

Another option to earn a profit as an affiliate marketer is to start generating your own products and/or services to promote to your audience too. As you work with your audience and earn consumers owing to the items you push and the information you post, you may obtain insight into the audience that gives you the idea to build a brand-new product for them. Your product might be free or for a cost, depending on how you're going to utilize it.

• Offering Bonuses

One method that you may add your own items to the mix is by giving a bonus for the purchase of a separate product for which you are an affiliate. The additional product allows you the option to add them to your list, raise your earnings, and perhaps illustrate more of what you can do for the audience about their problems.

Some affiliate systems allow you to add your additional product straight to their funnel on the affiliate platform (such as is given by aMember.com or JVZoo.com) if the product creator enables that feature for you. In other circumstances, you may have to be creative and deliver the bonus another method. However, there is a lot of technology that will do it automatically for you too.

• Building Your List

As an affiliate marketer, you may manufacture your own items that are purely for listbuilding reasons. A excellent example may be a checklist to assist your audience choose the proper affiliate marketing software or help them set up their first webinar.

Anything that your audience actually needs and wants that is easy to develop makes a great list builder.

• Another Income Stream

Additionally, as a product developer you may generate items as a distinct revenue stream over and above your money generating as an affiliate. Maybe you can develop a better cleaning organizing calendar than the one that you've been pushing.

Perhaps you have created a course on keeping your house organized that you want to promote. Once you produce the goods, you also may recruit affiliates to generate the sales for you.

As a product developer, you'll need to ensure that you have the correct software like aMember.com that allows you set up a shopping cart and even a membership site that enables you to distribute your digital items and services to your audience.

You may also utilize any number of affiliate networks listed to sell your items and recruit affiliates to improve your revenue.

Chapter 3

FINDING THE RIGHT AFFILIATES(AND WHICH TO AVOID)

Once you have created your own items that are available for purchase, it is necessary to establish your own affiliate network so that you may reach the most number of people possible. When you have your own affiliate network, it is the same as having a large number of salesmen working on your website every single day to expand your company. However, it does need some serious research and study in order to locate the appropriate affiliates.

• Prioritize quality above quantity

If your affiliates are not skilled salesmen, having a thousand of them will not be of any use to you. If the individuals who wish to market your goods use unethical methods to create sales, this may also have a very negative impact on you. You are able to avoid the majority of the issues that are associated with affiliates, including fraud and spam, if you place more of an emphasis on recruiting quality affiliates rather than a large number of affiliates. They have a website.

You should look at the websites of any candidates. To what extent do they maintain a blog? Does the material fit your audience? Is the website secure? Are they obeying all the essential laws for their nation and yours about spam, privacy, and other issues? Do they appear honest and confident based on the facts you see on the website?

• Their Domain Name

One technique to find out about the person behind the website is to run a "Who Is" search. Some of the websites are going to have the information obscured. If that occurs, do a bit extra investigation on to confirm that the folks behind the site are honest people who you'd like to work with in person.

• Their Content and Information

When you go to the site and read the material and information, does it speak to your audience such that they will prefer to purchase from them? What type of keywords do they use? Is the material and information direct and above board? Would you feel confident sending your mother to that site to acquire information?

• Financial Validation

The second thing you will want to do when you have an affiliate is to verify that they fill out all the necessary legal documents needed. Even if you are not going to send out 1099s because you pay via third party like PayPal, having that information is still important since it proves their legitimacy and verifies them in a manner that helps you keep your clients secure. Additionally, have they proved themselves to be good affiliate marketers?

When you are just starting out as a product seller, you may not be able to be too picky about who joins affiliates, but at the very least guarantee that they are who they say they are, that they are not criminals, and that they service their consumers honestly and openly. Just know that if you pick individuals who are new to affiliate marketing, you need to give training and encouragement to them so that they generate more sales.

Chapter 4

AFFLIATE MARKETING TECHNOLOGY

There are tools and technology that will make your work simpler after you have decided to become an affiliate marketer. These tools and technology will make your job easier. Tools for developing websites, tools for email marketing, tools for doing market research, and other types of tools are all examples of the technology that is already accessible.

• Tools for Websites

You need to choose the appropriate sort of domain name, hosting, website builder, and landing page automation in order to construct a website that has a high conversion rate. This will allow you to do more with less effort and with less emotional distress. The tools that are listed below will assist you in completing everything.

•Name of the Domain

To get started with your affiliate marketing income, one of the first things you need to do is get a domain name. This will allow you to construct a website that is appealing to the people who are most likely to be interested in your products or services. Make sure that the name you choose has a keyword, that it is brief and simple to remember, and that it has a dot-com extension. Namecheap.com is an amazing option worth considering when looking to purchase domains at a low cost.

The Hosting of Websites

The next thing you're going to need when you get your domain name is website hosting. You may want to check with the host before you purchase your name, since sometimes companies offer a deal where you receive the domain free by paying up ahead for hosting. A excellent website host delivers at least 99 percent uptime, strong customer service, and an easy to use website. A fantastic pick, particularly if you're a newbie and don't comprehend what you're doing, is MomWebs.com. They have great customer care and service.

• Website Builder

You also need to establish or have a strong affiliate website built. One of the finest and most utilized solutions for this is self-hosted WordPress. You may learn more about it at WordPress.org. (Note: This is not the same as WordPress.com, however that dot com is operated using self-hosted WordPress.) This builder is simple to use, affordable or even free, and what is most essential is that it performs brilliantly and search engines still love WordPress.

• Landing Page Builder

Once you have everything done, you're going to require some type of landing page builder. Now, you can accomplish this for free using self-hosted WordPress merely by establishing a new page, but it won't have as much automation on it.

One thing that might help you generate more money is automation so that you don't have to do everything manually. A solid alternative for automated landing page software is Instapage.com. If you utilize a powerful system like Infusionsoft.com for your marketing, you already have everything incorporated. This form of software will automate your funnels in a way that will appear to convert your site into an ATM some days.

• Email Marketing

Email marketing is not something you can miss out on. It's one of the most powerful and beneficial kinds of marketing that exists today. Even social media marketing cannot equal the potency of email marketing. This implies you're going to need to both acquire leads and send out emails automatically. One of the most popular choices nowadays is AWeber.com however there is also a lot of affection for ConvertKit.com and ActiveCampaign.com. These, together with your landing page builder, will automate so much.

• Market Research As an affiliate marketer, you're going to have to conduct a lot of market research to ensure your efforts do not go useless. If you don't conduct the research, you'll take a lot of action that is not going to create results. Don't make assumptions; do the research. You can investigate your competition using tools like iSpionage.com, and you can research hot subjects using something like Google Trends.

• Traffic Generation

Investing in technologies to aid with traffic creation is also a vital strategy to establish a successful affiliate marketing firm. After all, you need a lot of focused visitors to accomplish the outcomes you expected when you established your goals and objectives.

22.AdEspresso.com by Hootsuite – If you intend to run a lot of advertising on social media, this software is something that is going to assist you make it simpler. You'll be able to run advertisements that are gorgeous and optimized on all the leading social media platforms.

23.Facebook Ads – You may utilize Facebook directly to execute retargeting and remarketing campaigns by employing the Facebook pixel on your site. Then you run an ad that only previous visitors see, which has been demonstrated to boost traffic and revenue.

24.RecurPost.com – This program, once set up, will take your blog entries and push them out to the social networking sites you propose randomly and automatically.

Don't forget to send an email out too. When you have a new blog post, go ahead and inform your email audience about it utilizing your email marketing software's automatic blog post sharing tools.

• Tracking and Converting

The other tools you need to help you become a lucrative affiliate marketer are tools that assist you monitor the efficacy of your efforts and convert your audience. Every website has to install Google Analytics. It's free and it works great. After all, Google is still the dominant search engine. That implies you need to follow their instructions.

For link tracking, a nice option is PrettyLinks.com. You may build up your website so that each time you mention specified phrases, the program automatically inserts a affiliate link in that term. That's a terrific approach to automate your suggestions and measure clicks and conversions.

• Content Marketing

One of the methods you're going to produce more traffic for your ideal target audience is to post content that they'll be interested in. In order to develop captivating content, you'll need to complete your research, ensuring it's intelligible, and that it's attractive. Not only that - you also want to guarantee that you are providing material on a consistent and frequent basis. These tools can help you do that.

25.Research - When you want to perform research, the most obvious place to go is of course Google Search and Google Website Tools. That is where you should start. But there is also fantastic commercial software that you may use even more effectively depending on what you are investigating. A few methods you may want to attempt include social networking platform searches, rival searches, and their internal data via purchasing their goods.

26.Editing - When you publish something, whether it's a blog post or a product, you want to guarantee that it's legible to your audience. To do that, first you need to know who the audience is and what terminology they prefer using, then you need to be fluent in the language or employ someone who can assist.

You may also utilize programs like Grammarly.com to assist you edit. However, the main difficulty is that if you don't know what is correct, the program might mislead you.

27.Graphics - At some time, you'll want to make graphics to add more appeal to blog articles, social media updates, to generate eBooks and more. A excellent option for a non-graphic designer is to try Canva.com, however there is worth in employing an expert graphic designer to do that for you too.

28.Scheduling - There is a lot to accomplish when it comes to marketing and scheduling, as well as preparing what you are going to do to promote your affiliate company.

But software like CoSchedule.com can assist; this is a whole marketing suite that features a marketing calendar, a content organizer, social organizer, and more all in one area.

You may also need to employ someone to assist you plan and develop content for your affiliate company. You don't have to do everything yourself. You may engage a content writer to assist, and you can also utilize private label rights material to help you fill in the gaps in your content.

Using helpful technology that is created for marketers is a critical approach to go forward as an affiliate marketer. Always check the small print for any device you intend to purchase or use, since some of them specifically ban activities that involve affiliate marketing. It's always excellent habit to study the guidelines since it'll also provide you complete insight on utilizing each tool you acquire.

Chapter 5

MARKETING FOR MORE SALES AND PROFIT

As an affiliate marketer, it's going to become evident that the term, "always be marketing" applies to you in a significant way. For the word to go out about the solutions you are promoting, you have to inform people and promote. Thankfully there are numerous methods that you may market your affiliate company that are not expensive, and some are even free other than the time it takes to accomplish them.

Remember that you may have multiple components of your company to sell too. You will need to promote your own affiliate program to folks who would desire to earn money. You will need to promote the things you develop or locate to people who need them. Therefore, it's a business to company and business to consumer issue, and they should be promoted wholly independently from one another.

You can promote both in the same manner, but the content will seem different dependent on the audience and the product you're advertising. The major technique to promote your business is via content marketing.

• Content Marketing

This form of marketing involves any kind of marketing you are doing with content - including social media marketing, blogging, and email marketing. Create a strategy for every single product that you wish to market. Know who you're writing the content for, where it will appear, and what the call to action should be.

• Search Engine Optimization

Learn much you can about SEO since it's vital for your success. It will help you write better headlines, better subject lines, and indeed much better material that is targeted appropriately. Remember that SEO involves both on-page and off-page options - from internal link building to acquiring links to your work, and all should be considered. Adding tools like Yoast SEO to your blog may assist a lot.

• Paid Marketing

The most successful affiliate marketers employ paid promotion in addition to the free choices. Remember that there truly isn't any free choice, however. You'll either utilize your own time or your own money. Which you select relies on the priorities you have and the talents you possess.

• Social Media Marketing

Develop each platform that you use so that it reveals your brand voice and the image you want to portray on the globe. Use the information you make to get the word out to the public frequently - utilizing both free and paid solutions.

• Email Marketing

Email marketing is part of content marketing, but it has to be highlighted that email marketing is not something you can omit if you want to be a successful affiliate marketer long term. Building your own list based on your target demographic is what's going to keep you in business, even when your ideal audience expands and changes with time and social media sites fade out.

• Affiliates We have spoke about launching your own affiliate network to sell your own products that you produce depending on what your audience requires. This is a wonderful way to build buzz and get the word out quicker about any product you manufacture.

Once you have your own items, try bringing on affiliates. Start with your happiest clients and teach them to be excellent money-generating affiliates.

• Joint Venture Partnerships

One strategy to promote your company is to develop relationships with companies who serve the same audience as you do with similar goods and services. By the way, these are also possibilities for you to market their items as an affiliate and vice versa.

The way a JV works is that you agree to work together for a shared cause on a temporary or long-term basis, while staying separate companies for everything outside the joint endeavor. For example, you may get together with a number of your friends with affiliate programs, who provide programs to working parents with school-age kids such as food planning, home management, self-improvement and more.

You may put on a webinar with a few different specialists in this field, each providing their own product or service to the audience. Everyone advertises the event together at the same time to create hype. Then you broadcast the webinar live, and you may even replay it as live to attract even more leads.

The only way to earn more sales and profit is to promote more. Get more people involved and guarantee that as many people as possible are talking about your products and services. Don't be scared to actively inform your audience about your offers. After all, you know they work, and you are proud of them. Why wouldn't you tell others about them as much as you can?

Chapter 6

THE STEPS TO GETTING STARTED

Every successful enterprise begins with studying and then planning. Use this getting started list to help you genuinely get organized and take that first step toward affiliate marketing income.

1. Know Your Audience - Conduct research so that you know as much as you can about your audience. Where do they hang out? What keeps people awake at night. Who do they appreciate obtaining info from?

2. Know Your Audience's Pain problems – What are at least three pain problems that you can remedy using your expertise and the items you have made or discovered?

3. Know Your Why – It's vital that you know why you care about this target audience and why you are the best person to identify or create the items that become solutions for them.

4. Create a Branded Website for Your Audience – Your branding is vital because it has to communicate to the audience in such a manner that they grasp what your brand stands for straight away.

5. Set Up Branded Social Platforms – The same with your social platforms; they should be branded appropriately so that everyone knows it's you.

6. Set Up Your Email Autoresponder — You cannot be successful without email marketing so start growing your list before you have any items, utilizing freebies and checklists and your blog to entice them.

7. Set Up Your Funnels - Use technology to automate your marketing funnels for each product that you are going to offer to them.

8. Fill Your Website and Social Media with Targeted Content — Set up your content marketing strategy based on each product, service, and issue that your audience has.

9. Find a Product to Promote — Knowing your target, locate high-quality items that you can be

proud to promote with firms who give top-notch customer care.

10. Become an Affiliate for That Product – Sign up as an affiliate if you can discover the information to contact them about it. Don't quit up if you were turned down at first; build yourself up and come back if required.

11. Create material Based on the Product – Remember to create material based on the items you want to market to everyone depending on their stage in the purchasing journey.

12. Promote the material Everywhere — Use technology to promote your material everywhere, even when it's free. Promote it as if it's the most costly thing you have.

13. Check Your Numbers - Always keep examining your numbers to ensure that the actions you do receive the outcomes you expected.

14. Repeat – Don't stop. Be consistent and keep doing it. Adjust depending on your metrics.

The only question now is, what are you waiting for? Affiliate marketing is a profitable career to start, even on a part-time basis. You don't have to accomplish it all today. Start from the beginning and work your way through the procedure. Before you realize it, you'll start seeing the first revenue trickle into your bank account.